DOG BREEDS

Chihuahuas

by Sara Green

Consultant:
Michael Leuthner, D.V.M.
PetCare Clinic, Madison, Wisc.

BLASTOFF! READERS
4

BELLWETHER MEDIA • MINNEAPOLIS, MN

Note to Librarians, Teachers, and Parents:

Blastoff! Readers are carefully developed by literacy experts and combine standards-based content with developmentally appropriate text.

Level 1 provides the most support through repetition of high-frequency words, light text, predictable sentence patterns, and strong visual support.

Level 2 offers early readers a bit more challenge through varied simple sentences, increased text load, and less repetition of high-frequency words.

Level 3 advances early-fluent readers toward fluency through increased text and concept load, less reliance on visuals, longer sentences, and more literary language.

Level 4 builds reading stamina by providing more text per page, increased use of punctuation, greater variation in sentence patterns, and increasingly challenging vocabulary.

Level 5 encourages children to move from "learning to read" to "reading to learn" by providing even more text, varied writing styles, and less familiar topics.

Whichever book is right for your reader, Blastoff! Readers are the perfect books to build confidence and encourage a love of reading that will last a lifetime!

This edition first published in 2010 by Bellwether Media, Inc.

No part of this publication may be reproduced in whole or in part without written permission of the publisher. For information regarding permission, write to Bellwether Media, Inc., Attention: Permissions Department, 5357 Penn Avenue South, Minneapolis, MN 55419.

Library of Congress Cataloging-in-Publication Data
Green, Sara, 1964–
Chihuahuas / by Sara Green.
    p. cm. – (Blastoff! readers dog breeds)
Includes bibliographical references and index.
    Summary: "Simple text and full-color photography introduce beginning readers to the characteristics of the dog breed Chihuahuas. Developed by literacy experts for students in kindergarten through third grade"–Provided by publisher.
ISBN 978-1-60014-298-7 (hardcover : alk. paper)
1. Chihuahua (Dog breed)–Juvenile literature. I. Title.
SF429.C45G74 2010
636.76–dc22
                            2009037208

Printed in the United States of America, North Mankato, MN.
010110   1149

Contents

What Are Chihuahuas?

Chihuahuas are a small **breed** of dog with large, perky ears. They are a **toy breed**. Dogs in this group weigh less than 10 pounds (4.5 kilograms).

Adult Chihuahuas weigh 2 to 6 pounds (1 to 3 kilograms). They are 6 to 9 inches (15 to 23 centimeters) tall. The Chihuahua is the smallest toy breed in the world.

fun fact

In 2005, a 6-inch (15-centimeter) long Chihuahua was named the "smallest dog in terms of length" by the Guinness Book of World Records.

Chihuahua **coats** come in two different types. These are called smooth coat and long coat. **Litters** of puppies can have long coats and smooth coats.

Chihuahua coats come in many colors.
The most common colors are tan, black,
and brown. Their coats can be solid,
marked, or splashed.

Apple head

Chihuahuas have heads that are either called apple heads or deer heads.

Chihuahuas with deer heads have longer noses. Chihuahuas with apple heads have rounder heads.

Deer head

History of Chihuahuas

The **ancestor** of the Chihuahua breed was the **Techichi**. Techichis were short dogs with long coats. They lived over 2,000 years ago in Mexico and Central America.

Mexico

Central America

They were **companion dogs** to the **Toltec** people. The Toltecs believed the Techichis guided spirits to the afterlife.

Spanish explorers came to Mexico and Central America in the 1500s. They brought their dogs with them. One of the breeds was the Chinese Crested dog. Chinese Crested dogs are small and mostly hairless.

Chinese Crested dog

Many people think that the Techichis bred
with these dogs. Their puppies were probably
the first Chihuahuas.

The breed got the name Chihuahua in 1850. People from the United States discovered the breed in the Mexican state of Chihuahua. The people named the dogs after the state.

Chihuahua

Mexico

People in the United States liked
Chihuahuas. They became popular pets
by the early 1900s.

Chihuahuas Today

Chihuahuas are active dogs. Chihuahuas do well in a sport called **Teacup agility**. A Teacup agility course is a playground for small dogs.

It has tunnels, ramps, and hoops.
Owners teach Chihuahuas how to run
quickly through the course.

Many owners give their Chihuahuas Canine Good Citizen training. This training teaches Chihuahuas how to behave with people and other dogs. They learn how to stay calm in crowds.

fun fact

Chihuahuas often shiver. This does not always mean they are cold. They also shiver when they are excited or nervous.

Chihuahuas that pass the Canine Good Citizen test earn a certificate. They can also wear a Canine Good Citizen dog tag.

Chihuahuas have been companions to people for a long time. They are devoted to their owners. Their small size makes them easy to carry around. Some Chihuahua owners bring their Chihuahuas with them wherever they go!

Chihuahuas love to play. They also love to cuddle with their owners. Chihuahuas are small dogs with big personalities!

Glossary

ancestor—a family member who lived long ago

breed—a type of dog

coat—the hair or fur of an animal

companion dogs—dogs that provide friendship to people

litter—a group of young born from one mother at the same time

Teacup agility—a sport for small dogs where they run through a series of obstacles

Techichi—a dog breed that is one of the ancestors of Chihuahuas

Toltec—a civilization that once existed in Central America and southern Mexico

toy breed—a breed of dog that weighs less than 10 pounds (4.5 kilograms)

To Learn More

AT THE LIBRARY
American Kennel Club. *The Complete Dog Book for Kids*. New York, N.Y.: Howell Books, 1996.

Miller, Connie C. *Chihuahuas*. Mankato, Minn: Pebble Books, 2009.

Temple, Bob. *Chihuahuas*. Edina, Minn: Checkerboard Books, 2001.

ON THE WEB
Learning more about Chihuahuas is as easy as 1, 2, 3.

1. Go to www.factsurfer.com.

2. Enter "Chihuahuas" into the search box.

3. Click the "Surf" button and you will see a list of related Web sites.

With factsurfer.com, finding more information is just a click away.

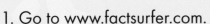

Index